My MoteNote

A <u>Mot</u>ivational <u>Note</u>book and Student Planner

LEARNINGFOUNDATIONS

Thank you to all the Learning Foundations' students who helped shape this book and taught us that it takes great learners to be great teachers!

This book is dedicated to our own amazing teens who were test-subjects and who keep us accountable for talking the walk and walking the talk.
Ethan, Cadyn, Addi, Seth, Reis, and Sadie –

We love and appreciate you. Thank you!

Jennifer Price, M.S.
Pamela Iken, M.A.

Contributing Author:
Cindy Garza

My MoteNote™, ©2021 Learning Foundations, LLC.

My MoteNote

A <u>Mot</u>ivational <u>Note</u>book and Student Planner JUST FOR YOU!

Your life is dynamic and full of change. As your body, heart, and brain grow exponentially, so do your ideas, feelings, and worries. This **MoteNote** is designed to be a compass to your best self as it inspires, motivates, and teaches you meaningful ways to focus, plan, and create at school and at home. Take your **MoteNote** everywhere! It includes:

- Organization and Time Management Tools
- Emotional Coping Strategies
- Words of Wisdom and Inspiration
- Fun and Creativity
- Academic Study Skills
- Handy Math Resources

This is YOUR **MoteNote**, so add colors, designs, and your unique style. Enjoy making this planner your own! This **MoteNote** is a powerful tool just as it is. However, with Educational Coaching from Learning Foundations to guide you through each page, it will become even more impactful! Connect with a Learning Foundations' coach, and listen to our podcasts by visiting <u>learningfoundations.org</u>.

Designed to fill in the GAP, Your MoteNote will lead you to…
"<u>G</u>row, <u>A</u>chieve, and <u>P</u>revail!"

Table of Contents

Each month, your **MoteNote** features these tools to <u>BOOST YOUR ORGANIZATIONAL SUPERPOWERS</u>:

- Monthly Calendars
- A Visual Snapshot of Your Time Each Day
- Cool Challenges, Fun Facts, and Personal Reflection Questions

Each month, there is one exercise in each of these categories <u>TO BRING OUT THE GENIUS IN YOU</u>:

- Organization and Time Management Tools
- Emotional Coping Strategies
- Words of Wisdom and Inspiration
- Fun and Creativity

The last two sections of your **MoteNote** will prepare you to <u>BE THE SMARTEST PERSON IN THE ROOM</u>:

- Academic Study Skills > Pages 122 - 130
- Handy Math Resources > Pages 132 - 138

Month:

Sunday	Monday	Tuesday	Wednesday

Thursday	Friday	Saturday

▶ To Do:

▶ Reminders:

Visual Snapshot of Your Week

KNOW how you spend time? Track your days. SEE **the truth!**

| | Get Ready for School | Morning School | Lunch Break | Afternoon School | Homework | Dinner Break and Leave for Soccer | Soccer Practice | Go Home, Wind Down | Sleep |

Example: 6 7 8 9 10 11 12 1 2 3 4 5 6 7 8 9 10 11 12

Sunday: 6 7 8 9 10 11 12 1 2 3 4 5 6 7 8 9 10 11 12

Monday: 6 7 8 9 10 11 12 1 2 3 4 5 6 7 8 9 10 11 12

Tuesday: 6 7 8 9 10 11 12 1 2 3 4 5 6 7 8 9 10 11 12

Wednesday: 6 7 8 9 10 11 12 1 2 3 4 5 6 7 8 9 10 11 12

Thursday: 6 7 8 9 10 11 12 1 2 3 4 5 6 7 8 9 10 11 12

Friday: 6 7 8 9 10 11 12 1 2 3 4 5 6 7 8 9 10 11 12

Saturday: 6 7 8 9 10 11 12 1 2 3 4 5 6 7 8 9 10 11 12

Monthly Personal Reflection

Use the exercises below to reflect upon last month and prepare for the month ahead. Also, enjoy "Fun Facts" and share them with your friends!

List 5 things you were **GRATEFUL** for this month:

1. _____
2. _____
3. _____
4. _____
5. _____

CHALLENGE yourself! Check out these ideas:

Try out a new hobby. You may like it, you may not, but at least you will have tried something new!

****

Compliment 3 important people in your life!

Share these **FUN FACTS** with a friend today:

- In 1989, Pepsi had the 6th largest military force in the world due to a trade agreement with the USSR.

- The only English letter not used in any US state name is 'Q'.

- Wombat poop is always cube-shaped.

- The first Disney character was Oswald the Lucky Rabbit. Five years later, Mickey Mouse was created, but he was originally named Mortimer Mouse.

THINK ABOUT

What went well last month?

What could have gone better?

What did I learn?

What will I do differently?

Login Information

Got your passwords written on the back of your hand or on a sticky note somewhere? Tired of resetting your Username or Password?

If you use the same password all the time - STOP! Cyber bullies are extremely dangerous, so protect your privacy and keep all your login info stored in one place, right here!

APP / WEBSITE	USERNAME	PASSWORD

Your SENSES are your Superpowers!

Your senses are powerful tools to help you navigate the world around you. They help you absorb, store, and remember information. They also help you adjust and cope with challenges and new experiences.

Slow down and engage your senses using the following process:

Name <u>6 things</u> you are **thinking** or **feeling** right now

Name <u>5 things</u> you can **see** right now

Name <u>4 things</u> you can **hear** right now

Name <u>3 things</u> you can **touch** right now

Name <u>2 things</u> you can **smell** right now

Name <u>1 thing</u> you can **taste** right now

Discover Your Learning Style
Optimize *HOW YOU LEARN*

Why is your Learning Style important?

You learn about the world around you through your senses! You use your eyes, ears, hands, mouth, and heart to make sense of information. You also use your senses to lock in memories and long-term learning.

Your Learning Style is how your brain is naturally wired to learn and remember. The more senses you use to learn, the longer you will remember it.

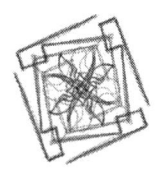

How Do You Remember Best?

VISUAL VERBAL | VISUAL PICTURES | AUDITORY | RELATIONAL | KINESTHETIC

Do you use words, images, or sounds to remember someone's name?
When you tell a story, do you describe what people were wearing or what they did?
When you need to remember something important, do you say it out loud or write it down?

These are your Learning Style preferences. They connect you to the world.
Pay attention to what your brain needs to learn and remember!

Your Playlist

Some songs cheer us up, others help us release stress. Some chill us out, others energize us. Make your playlist here, and pick songs from the list when you need a mood change.

Month:

Sunday	Monday	Tuesday	Wednesday

Thursday	Friday	Saturday

▶ To Do:
....
....
....
....
....
....
....

▶ Reminders:
....
....
....
....
....
....

Visual Snapshot of Your Week

KNOW how you spend time? Track your days. SEE **the truth!**

	Get Ready for School	Morning School	Lunch Break	Afternoon School	Homework	Dinner Break and Leave for Soccer	Soccer Practice	Go Home, Wind Down	Sleep

Example — | 6 | 7 | 8 | 9 | 10 | 11 | 12 | 1 | 2 | 3 | 4 | 5 | 6 | 7 | 8 | 9 | 10 | 11 | 12 |

Sunday — | 6 | 7 | 8 | 9 | 10 | 11 | 12 | 1 | 2 | 3 | 4 | 5 | 6 | 7 | 8 | 9 | 10 | 11 | 12 |

Monday — | 6 | 7 | 8 | 9 | 10 | 11 | 12 | 1 | 2 | 3 | 4 | 5 | 6 | 7 | 8 | 9 | 10 | 11 | 12 |

Tuesday — | 6 | 7 | 8 | 9 | 10 | 11 | 12 | 1 | 2 | 3 | 4 | 5 | 6 | 7 | 8 | 9 | 10 | 11 | 12 |

Wednesday — | 6 | 7 | 8 | 9 | 10 | 11 | 12 | 1 | 2 | 3 | 4 | 5 | 6 | 7 | 8 | 9 | 10 | 11 | 12 |

Thursday — | 6 | 7 | 8 | 9 | 10 | 11 | 12 | 1 | 2 | 3 | 4 | 5 | 6 | 7 | 8 | 9 | 10 | 11 | 12 |

Friday — | 6 | 7 | 8 | 9 | 10 | 11 | 12 | 1 | 2 | 3 | 4 | 5 | 6 | 7 | 8 | 9 | 10 | 11 | 12 |

Saturday — | 6 | 7 | 8 | 9 | 10 | 11 | 12 | 1 | 2 | 3 | 4 | 5 | 6 | 7 | 8 | 9 | 10 | 11 | 12 |

Monthly Personal Reflection

Use the exercises below to reflect upon last month and prepare for the month ahead. Also, enjoy "Fun Facts" and share them with your friends!

List 5 things you were **GRATEFUL** for this month:

1. _____
2. _____
3. _____
4. _____
5. _____

CHALLENGE yourself! Check out these ideas:

Visit a new restaurant and order something unique from the menu.

****

Watch a movie from the 60's, 70's, 80's, or 90's.

Share these **FUN FACTS** with a friend today:

- In a room with 23 people, there is a 50% chance that at least 2 people share a birthday!

- Nothing with mass can exceed the speed of light which is 30,000,000 m/s.

- The author of "Mary Had a Little Lamb", Sarah Josepha Hale, is also responsible for making Thanksgiving a national holiday in America.

- In 1992, Abraham Lincoln was inducted into the wrestling hall of fame for having only one loss in over 300 bouts.

THINK ABOUT

- What went well last month?
- What could have gone better?
- What did I learn?
- What will I do differently?

Your Morning (A.M.) Routine
TRACKING MY MORNING ROUTINE WITH VISUAL TIME

Directions: Estimate the time it will take you to complete each of the morning tasks below. Then use the clock to draw in these estimations, and utilize the 5-minute markers to help you form a pie chart to see your plan and time visually.

Use colors and/or pictures to represent your time visually on the clock.

▶ ESTIMATIONS:
- Wake up at _____
- Brush teeth (___ mins)
- Shower (___ mins)
- Get clothes (___ mins)
- Hair (___ mins)
- Breakfast (___ mins)
- Grab stuff (___ mins)
- Drive time (___ mins)
- Other (___ mins)

▶ Your estimates show it will take you ___ minutes to complete your morning routine and arrive at your destination. Were you correct?

What Bugs You?

On the lines below, list things that bug you. By recognizing what sets you off, you can be prepared to react calmly.

- _____
- _____
- _____
- _____
- _____

What do YOU do that Bugs Others?

Identify how you annoy others. (Believe it or not, you can be annoying! We all can!) Be aware of these nuances so you can minimize them.

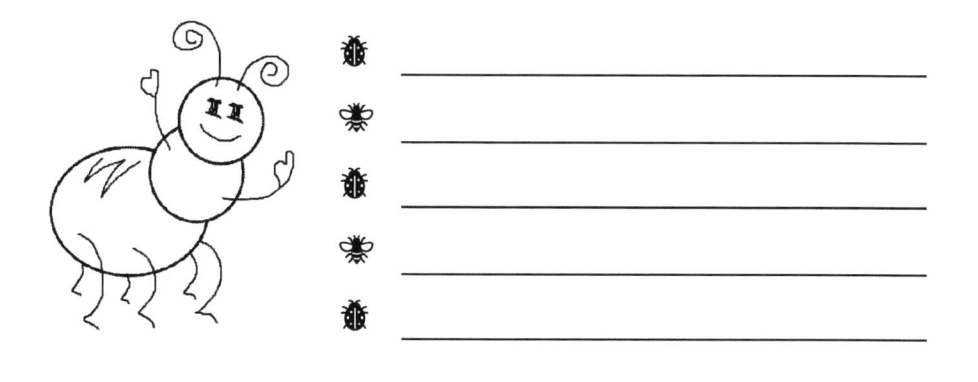

- _____
- _____
- _____
- _____
- _____

" Inspirational Quotes "

" Joy is the result of being grateful for what we have. "

" In a world of adventures, there's no time to be bored. "

" You learn nothing in life if you think you know everything. "

" If you're always trying to be normal, you'll never know how amazing you can be. "

" On especially tough days, I like to remind myself that my track record for getting through bad days so far is 100%, and that's pretty good. "

"   "

"   "

"   "

"   "

"   "

"   "

"   "

"   "

"   "

"   "

☆ Personal Stats ☆

Use colors to track how you rate in the following areas.
Challenge yourself to grow in areas of weakness.

Funny/Humorous:	1	2	3	4	5	6	7	8	9	10
Witty/Clever:	1	2	3	4	5	6	7	8	9	10
Book Smart:	1	2	3	4	5	6	7	8	9	10
Street Smart:	1	2	3	4	5	6	7	8	9	10
Hard Working:	1	2	3	4	5	6	7	8	9	10
Easy Going:	1	2	3	4	5	6	7	8	9	10
Compassionate:	1	2	3	4	5	6	7	8	9	10
Resilient:	1	2	3	4	5	6	7	8	9	10
Kind:	1	2	3	4	5	6	7	8	9	10
Creative:	1	2	3	4	5	6	7	8	9	10
Perceptive:	1	2	3	4	5	6	7	8	9	10
Confident:	1	2	3	4	5	6	7	8	9	10
Cooperative:	1	2	3	4	5	6	7	8	9	10

Month:

Sunday	Monday	Tuesday	Wednesday

Thursday	Friday	Saturday

▶ To Do:

▶ Reminders:

Visual Snapshot of Your Week

KNOW how you spend time? Track your days. SEE **the truth!**

	Get Ready for School	Morning School	Lunch Break	Afternoon School	Homework	Dinner Break and Leave for Soccer	Soccer Practice	Go Home, Wind Down	Sleep

Example — | 6 | 7 | 8 | 9 | 10 | 11 | 12 | 1 | 2 | 3 | 4 | 5 | 6 | 7 | 8 | 9 | 10 | 11 | 12 |

Sunday — | 6 | 7 | 8 | 9 | 10 | 11 | 12 | 1 | 2 | 3 | 4 | 5 | 6 | 7 | 8 | 9 | 10 | 11 | 12 |

Monday — | 6 | 7 | 8 | 9 | 10 | 11 | 12 | 1 | 2 | 3 | 4 | 5 | 6 | 7 | 8 | 9 | 10 | 11 | 12 |

Tuesday — | 6 | 7 | 8 | 9 | 10 | 11 | 12 | 1 | 2 | 3 | 4 | 5 | 6 | 7 | 8 | 9 | 10 | 11 | 12 |

Wednesday — | 6 | 7 | 8 | 9 | 10 | 11 | 12 | 1 | 2 | 3 | 4 | 5 | 6 | 7 | 8 | 9 | 10 | 11 | 12 |

Thursday — | 6 | 7 | 8 | 9 | 10 | 11 | 12 | 1 | 2 | 3 | 4 | 5 | 6 | 7 | 8 | 9 | 10 | 11 | 12 |

Friday — | 6 | 7 | 8 | 9 | 10 | 11 | 12 | 1 | 2 | 3 | 4 | 5 | 6 | 7 | 8 | 9 | 10 | 11 | 12 |

Saturday — | 6 | 7 | 8 | 9 | 10 | 11 | 12 | 1 | 2 | 3 | 4 | 5 | 6 | 7 | 8 | 9 | 10 | 11 | 12 |

Monthly Personal Reflection

Use the exercises below to reflect upon last month and prepare for the month ahead. Also, enjoy "Fun Facts" and share them with your friends!

List 5 things you were **GRATEFUL** for this month:

1. _____
2. _____
3. _____
4. _____
5. _____

CHALLENGE yourself! Check out these ideas:

Have a meaningful conversation with your family and ask questions.

****

Start a new book you wouldn't normally read.

Share these **FUN FACTS** with a friend today:

- A 4-dimensional cube is called a "teseract" or "hyper cube."

- If we had a one minute moment of silence for every victim of the Holocaust, we would be silent for 11 years.

- A baby puffin is called a puffling.

- If every human in history shuffled a deck of cards 1,000,000 times a second from the beginning of time, we still would not know all of the possible card orderings.

THINK ABOUT

What went well last month?

What could have gone better?

What did I learn?

What will I do differently?

Wise Mind

Your Wise Mind is the space where your Emotional Mind and Logical Mind overlap. Wise people live in the Wise Mind.

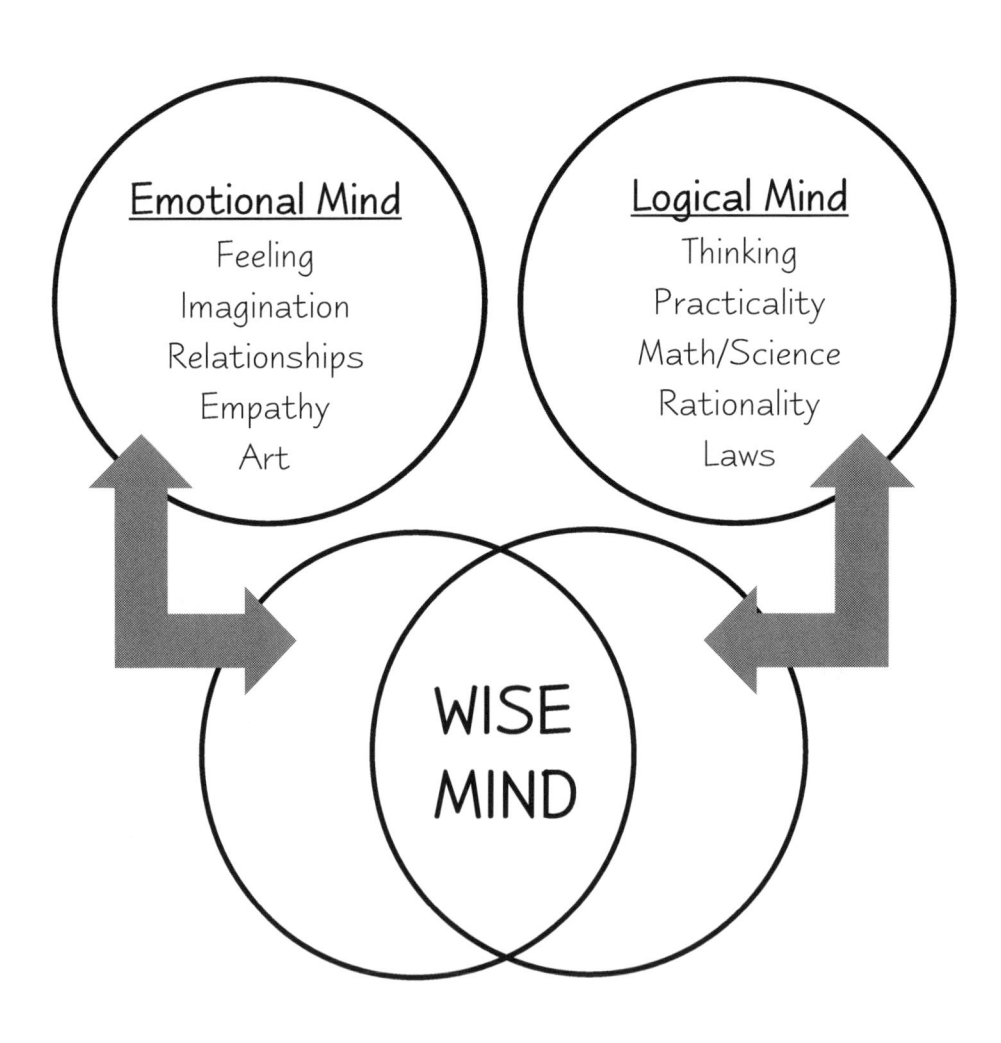

Emotional Mind
Feeling
Imagination
Relationships
Empathy
Art

Logical Mind
Thinking
Practicality
Math/Science
Rationality
Laws

WISE MIND

Who Can You Lean On?

SITUATION	WHO TO CALL	CONTACT INFORMATION

Laughter Truly is Great Medicine!

According to brain research, laughter produces a surge of endorphins with both euphoric and calming effects. Want to improve your mood, lessen your stress, and feel better overall?

LAUGH!

Take Time to Create

COLOR | SHADE | TRACE | BREATHE | RELAX

Month:

Sunday	Monday	Tuesday	Wednesday

Thursday	Friday	Saturday

▶ To Do:

▶ Reminders:

Visual Snapshot of Your Week

KNOW how you spend time? Track your days. SEE the truth!

Activity	Time
Get Ready for School	6–8
Morning School	8–12
Lunch Break	12–1
Afternoon School	1–3
Homework	3–5
Dinner Break and Leave for Soccer	5–7
Soccer Practice	7–9
Go Home, Wind Down	9–11
Sleep	11–12

Example | 6 | 7 | 8 | 9 | 10 | 11 | 12 | 1 | 2 | 3 | 4 | 5 | 6 | 7 | 8 | 9 | 10 | 11 | 12 |

Sunday | 6 | 7 | 8 | 9 | 10 | 11 | 12 | 1 | 2 | 3 | 4 | 5 | 6 | 7 | 8 | 9 | 10 | 11 | 12 |

Monday | 6 | 7 | 8 | 9 | 10 | 11 | 12 | 1 | 2 | 3 | 4 | 5 | 6 | 7 | 8 | 9 | 10 | 11 | 12 |

Tuesday | 6 | 7 | 8 | 9 | 10 | 11 | 12 | 1 | 2 | 3 | 4 | 5 | 6 | 7 | 8 | 9 | 10 | 11 | 12 |

Wednesday | 6 | 7 | 8 | 9 | 10 | 11 | 12 | 1 | 2 | 3 | 4 | 5 | 6 | 7 | 8 | 9 | 10 | 11 | 12 |

Thursday | 6 | 7 | 8 | 9 | 10 | 11 | 12 | 1 | 2 | 3 | 4 | 5 | 6 | 7 | 8 | 9 | 10 | 11 | 12 |

Friday | 6 | 7 | 8 | 9 | 10 | 11 | 12 | 1 | 2 | 3 | 4 | 5 | 6 | 7 | 8 | 9 | 10 | 11 | 12 |

Saturday | 6 | 7 | 8 | 9 | 10 | 11 | 12 | 1 | 2 | 3 | 4 | 5 | 6 | 7 | 8 | 9 | 10 | 11 | 12 |

Monthly Personal Reflection

Use the exercises below to reflect upon last month and prepare for the month ahead. Also, enjoy "Fun Facts" and share them with your friends!

List 5 things you were **GRATEFUL** for this month:

1. _____
2. _____
3. _____
4. _____
5. _____

CHALLENGE yourself! Check out these ideas:

Watch a movie from another country that's in a different language.

****

Listen to a new podcast about a topic you usually wouldn't listen to.

Share these **FUN FACTS** with a friend today:

➢ Pokémon is the highest grossing franchise in the world.

➢ Humans can't digest hair.

➢ Nearly 3% of the ice in Antarctica consists of penguin urine.

➢ Did you know you have brain cells in your heart and stomach too? It's true! This means there's a constant two-way dialogue between your brain (the first brain), your heart (the little brain), and your stomach (the second brain).

THINK ABOUT

What went well last month?

What could have gone better?

What did I learn?

What will I do differently?

I Am Many Things!

All over the star, jot down words that describe you. Think about your different roles, characteristics, and talents!

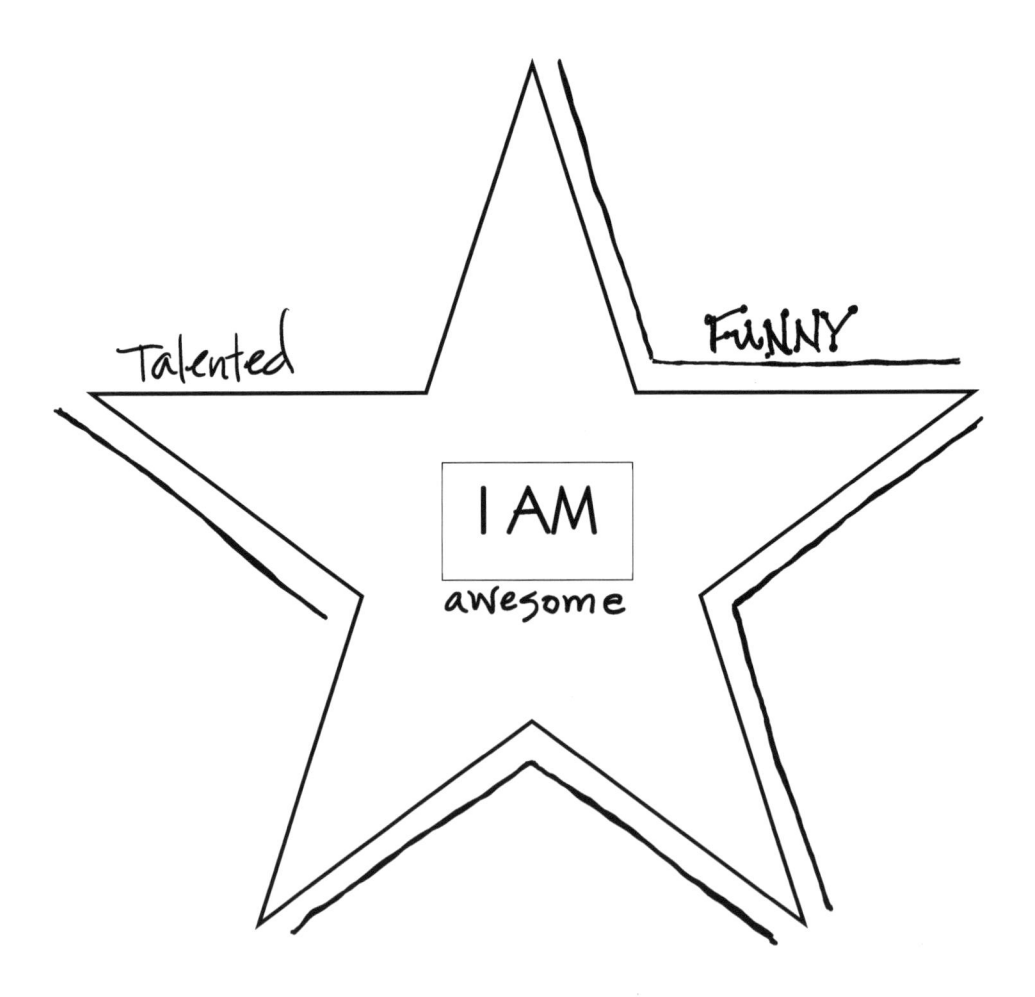

Talented

FUNNY

I AM

awesome

B.I.N.G.O.

WAYS TO CALM STRESS

Cross off each box after you've tried a new strategy!

Write out your thoughts	Remember good advice	Listen to music	Doodle	Limit social media
Replace the phrase, "I hate" with, "I can handle this"	Compliment someone	REPEAT: I am awesome; I am happy!	Complete the "I Am Many Things" page in your MoteNote	Read inspirational stories
Forgive yourself	Take 5 slow, deep breaths	★	Smile for 15 seconds straight	Repeat: "I can. So, I will."
List 3 beautiful things near you	STRETCH like a cat	Describe your perfect place	List 5 things you do well	Forgive others
List 5 things that make you happy	Put lavender oil on your temples	Ask for a hug	Give a hug	Write down how you feel
Use your MoteNote to track time and tasks	Hand in your homework	Take a 10 minute walk outside	Finish this sentence at least 5 times: "I can…"	Use your eyes, ears, and heart to hear others' opinions

Never Miss a Good Crisis

#teachablemoments

- A Normal Part of Life
- Teachable Moments
- How We Learn
- Life Lessons
- Powerful
- Valuable

Mistakes are...

Experience teaches us ALL lessons.
When we learn from them, we are wiser for it.

*** Be Wise! ***

Brain Dump

FEELING FRUSTRATED OR JUDGED?
LAY IT ALL OUT HERE, AND THEN LET IT GO!

WRITING IS A POWERFUL WAY TO SORT THROUGH COMPLEX FEELINGS AND THOUGHTS. REPLACE NEGATIVE THOUGHTS WITH POSITIVE THOUGHTS, AND YOU WILL QUICKLY FEEL LESS STRESSED.

Month:

Sunday	Monday	Tuesday	Wednesday

Thursday	Friday	Saturday

▶ To Do:

▶ Reminders:

Visual Snapshot of Your Week

KNOW how you spend time? Track your days. SEE **the truth!**

	Get Ready for School	Morning School	Lunch Break	Afternoon School	Homework	Dinner Break and Leave for Soccer	Soccer Practice	Go Home, Wind Down	Sleep

Example — | 6 | 7 | 8 | 9 | 10 | 11 | 12 | 1 | 2 | 3 | 4 | 5 | 6 | 7 | 8 | 9 | 10 | 11 | 12 |

Sunday — | 6 | 7 | 8 | 9 | 10 | 11 | 12 | 1 | 2 | 3 | 4 | 5 | 6 | 7 | 8 | 9 | 10 | 11 | 12 |

Monday — | 6 | 7 | 8 | 9 | 10 | 11 | 12 | 1 | 2 | 3 | 4 | 5 | 6 | 7 | 8 | 9 | 10 | 11 | 12 |

Tuesday — | 6 | 7 | 8 | 9 | 10 | 11 | 12 | 1 | 2 | 3 | 4 | 5 | 6 | 7 | 8 | 9 | 10 | 11 | 12 |

Wednesday — | 6 | 7 | 8 | 9 | 10 | 11 | 12 | 1 | 2 | 3 | 4 | 5 | 6 | 7 | 8 | 9 | 10 | 11 | 12 |

Thursday — | 6 | 7 | 8 | 9 | 10 | 11 | 12 | 1 | 2 | 3 | 4 | 5 | 6 | 7 | 8 | 9 | 10 | 11 | 12 |

Friday — | 6 | 7 | 8 | 9 | 10 | 11 | 12 | 1 | 2 | 3 | 4 | 5 | 6 | 7 | 8 | 9 | 10 | 11 | 12 |

Saturday — | 6 | 7 | 8 | 9 | 10 | 11 | 12 | 1 | 2 | 3 | 4 | 5 | 6 | 7 | 8 | 9 | 10 | 11 | 12 |

Monthly Personal Reflection

Use the exercises below to reflect upon last month and prepare for the month ahead. Also, enjoy "Fun Facts" and share them with your friends!

List 5 things you were **GRATEFUL** for this month:

1. _____
2. _____
3. _____
4. _____
5. _____

CHALLENGE yourself! Check out these ideas:

Instead of always texting, call a friend and have a conversation.

****

Enjoy listening to a new genre of music.

Share these **FUN FACTS** with a friend today:

- Dwayne "The Rock" Johnson is the first 3rd generation pro wrestler.

- The world's population standing shoulder to shoulder could fit within New York City.

- The first selfie, formerly called a photographic portrait, was taken in 1839 by Robert Cornelius.

- South Korea has 12 "love days" per year. Each day is celebrated differently, and themes include sharing flowers, photos, and cookies!

THINK ABOUT

What went well last month?

What could have gone better?

What did I learn?

What will I do differently?

Habit Tracker

List healthy habits and check off the days you practice them.

	Sunday	Monday	Tuesday	Wednesday	Thursday	Friday	Saturday
Brush teeth twice a day							
Eat breakfast							
Do homework without being told							
Get at least 8 hours of sleep							

Monthly Mood Tracker

Color in each day of the month with the main emotion you are feeling that day using the legend below. At the end of the month, reflect upon the patterns you see.

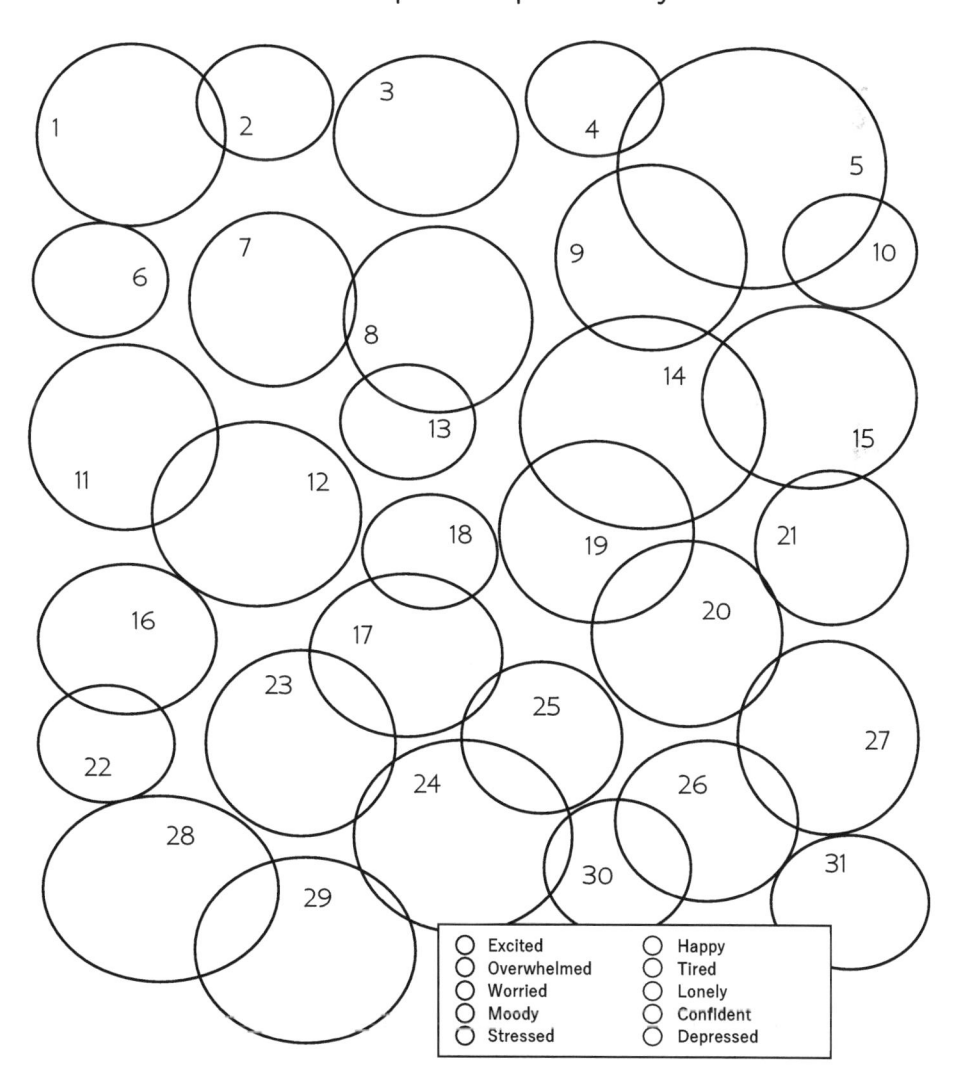

- ○ Excited
- ○ Overwhelmed
- ○ Worried
- ○ Moody
- ○ Stressed
- ○ Happy
- ○ Tired
- ○ Lonely
- ○ Confident
- ○ Depressed

Listen Before You Speak

BECAUSE <u>EVERYONE</u> IS GOING THROUGH SOMETHING TOUGH.

First, **THINK AND LISTEN**,
LISTEN with your heart.
Then, **SPEAK** to their heart,
and share your heart!

Listen, stay calm, and have compassion for others.

You're a Super Star!

Trace, color, and create to stay focused.
Fill in the star with YOUR SUPERPOWERS!

Month:

Sunday	Monday	Tuesday	Wednesday

Thursday	Friday	Saturday

To Do:

....
....
....
....
....
....
....

Reminders:

....
....
....
....
....
....

Visual Snapshot of Your Week

KNOW how you spend time? Track your days. SEE the truth!

Get Ready for School | Morning School | Lunch Break | Afternoon School | Homework | Dinner Break and Leave for Soccer | Soccer Practice | Go Home, Wind Down | Sleep

Example — | 6 | 7 | 8 | 9 | 10 | 11 | 12 | 1 | 2 | 3 | 4 | 5 | 6 | 7 | 8 | 9 | 10 | 11 | 12 |

Sunday — | 6 | 7 | 8 | 9 | 10 | 11 | 12 | 1 | 2 | 3 | 4 | 5 | 6 | 7 | 8 | 9 | 10 | 11 | 12 |

Monday — | 6 | 7 | 8 | 9 | 10 | 11 | 12 | 1 | 2 | 3 | 4 | 5 | 6 | 7 | 8 | 9 | 10 | 11 | 12 |

Tuesday — | 6 | 7 | 8 | 9 | 10 | 11 | 12 | 1 | 2 | 3 | 4 | 5 | 6 | 7 | 8 | 9 | 10 | 11 | 12 |

Wednesday — | 6 | 7 | 8 | 9 | 10 | 11 | 12 | 1 | 2 | 3 | 4 | 5 | 6 | 7 | 8 | 9 | 10 | 11 | 12 |

Thursday — | 6 | 7 | 8 | 9 | 10 | 11 | 12 | 1 | 2 | 3 | 4 | 5 | 6 | 7 | 8 | 9 | 10 | 11 | 12 |

Friday — | 6 | 7 | 8 | 9 | 10 | 11 | 12 | 1 | 2 | 3 | 4 | 5 | 6 | 7 | 8 | 9 | 10 | 11 | 12 |

Saturday — | 6 | 7 | 8 | 9 | 10 | 11 | 12 | 1 | 2 | 3 | 4 | 5 | 6 | 7 | 8 | 9 | 10 | 11 | 12 |

Monthly Personal Reflection

Use the exercises below to reflect upon last month and prepare for the month ahead. Also, enjoy "Fun Facts" and share them with your friends!

List 5 things you were **GRATEFUL** for this month:

1. _____
2. _____
3. _____
4. _____
5. _____

CHALLENGE yourself! Check out these ideas:

Learn a new word and use it in a conversation this week.

****

Do a quick workout at the start of each day.

Share these **FUN FACTS** with a friend today:

- All giant pandas in zoos are on loan from China.

- One million seconds is about 11.5 days, while one billion seconds is just over 31.7 YEARS!

- The word 'Kamikaze' means "divine winds" and comes from typhoons that protected Japan from Mongol attacks in 1274.

- Between the ages of 6-13 you need 10 hours of sleep, between 13-17 you need 9 hours, and between 18-25 you need 8 hours of sleep a night to function normally.

THINK ABOUT

What went well last month?

What could have gone better?

What did I learn?

What will I do differently?

Your LOCKER

Your locker is a powerful tool for organization and planning. Set it up with reminders, a calendar, to-do lists, and other helpful resources. Turn your locker into your second brain!

Want Life to be Better?
Turn negative thinking into positive thinking.

Every day, we think tens of thousands of thoughts. Unfortunately, our brains tend to think negative thoughts 80% of the time and repeat those thoughts over and over. Soon, we come to believe and act on our "Automatic Negative Thoughts."
- <u>Even when they're wrong</u>. -

What plays in your track? Are your thoughts riddled with worries, fears, or complaints? Do you balance your negative thoughts with positive, reassuring, and happy thoughts?
- <u>You should!</u> -

Set yourself up for success by thinking positively.
Positive thinking increases oxygen intake, blood flow, and releases dopamine in the brain.
- <u>Dopamine is a happy hormone</u>. -

<u>NEGATIVE THINKING:</u> Slows the brain down and releases cortisol, a stress hormone.	<u>POSITIVE THINKING:</u> Stimulates the brain and releases dopamine, a happy hormone.
"I hate math" changes to…	"I LOOOOVEEE math." "This is worth it. Math is important." "This chapter is tough, but I'll get it!" "I should ask for help in this section." "I won't give up on ME!"
"She hates me!" changes to…	"We should get to know each other." "We don't see eye to eye, but it's ok." "I bet we have something in common." "Not everybody has to like me."

Brain Hacks

Help your brain work better and faster with these Brain Hacks. Add your own!

When you want to get your creativity flowing, raise your eyebrows and widen your eyes. Taking more in allows ideas to grow!

Feeling stressed? Slowly, BREATHE in & out 5X. Then, SMILE for 30 seconds. Repeat until you feel better.

Stimulate two or more senses at the same time to remember things easier.

Do everyday tasks with your non-dominant hand to challenge and strengthen your brain and to build resiliency.

Don't make decisions when you feel emotional or mad. Sleep on it. Wait until you know which choice is the best option.

Map out your week by completing the VISUALIZE TIME log each month. Use colors to track how much you watch TV, read, or play games.

LAUGH! Fake laughter soon turns to real laughter, and you will feel better and think sharper.

Listen to music while you do the dishes or clean your room. This will help motivate you!

Great Job Showing Up Today!
You're Crushing It!!!

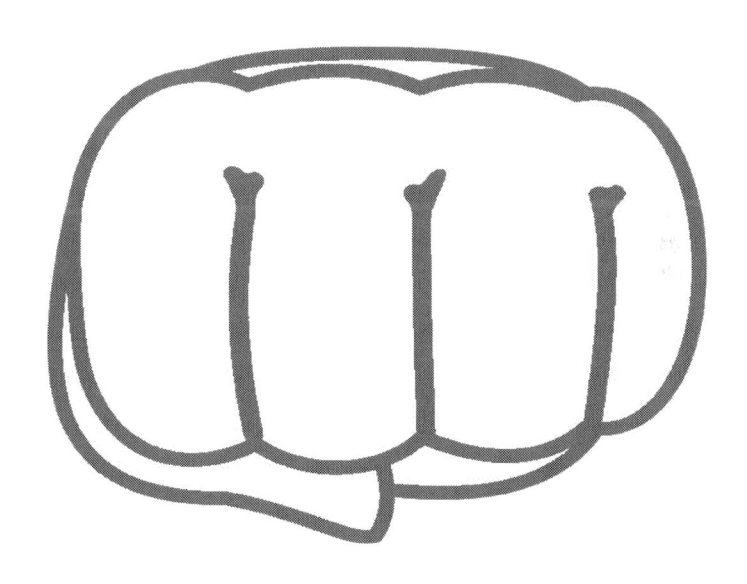

Fist bump, keep it up!

Month:

Sunday	Monday	Tuesday	Wednesday

Thursday	Friday	Saturday

▶ To Do:

▶ Reminders:

Visual Snapshot of Your Week

KNOW how you spend time? Track your days. SEE **the truth!**

Example

| Get Ready for School | Morning School | Lunch Break | Afternoon School | Homework | Dinner Break and Leave for Soccer | Soccer Practice | Go Home, Wind Down | Sleep |

| 6 | 7 | 8 | 9 | 10 | 11 | 12 | 1 | 2 | 3 | 4 | 5 | 6 | 7 | 8 | 9 | 10 | 11 | 12 |

Sunday
| 6 | 7 | 8 | 9 | 10 | 11 | 12 | 1 | 2 | 3 | 4 | 5 | 6 | 7 | 8 | 9 | 10 | 11 | 12 |

Monday
| 6 | 7 | 8 | 9 | 10 | 11 | 12 | 1 | 2 | 3 | 4 | 5 | 6 | 7 | 8 | 9 | 10 | 11 | 12 |

Tuesday
| 6 | 7 | 8 | 9 | 10 | 11 | 12 | 1 | 2 | 3 | 4 | 5 | 6 | 7 | 8 | 9 | 10 | 11 | 12 |

Wednesday
| 6 | 7 | 8 | 9 | 10 | 11 | 12 | 1 | 2 | 3 | 4 | 5 | 6 | 7 | 8 | 9 | 10 | 11 | 12 |

Thursday
| 6 | 7 | 8 | 9 | 10 | 11 | 12 | 1 | 2 | 3 | 4 | 5 | 6 | 7 | 8 | 9 | 10 | 11 | 12 |

Friday
| 6 | 7 | 8 | 9 | 10 | 11 | 12 | 1 | 2 | 3 | 4 | 5 | 6 | 7 | 8 | 9 | 10 | 11 | 12 |

Saturday
| 6 | 7 | 8 | 9 | 10 | 11 | 12 | 1 | 2 | 3 | 4 | 5 | 6 | 7 | 8 | 9 | 10 | 11 | 12 |

Monthly Personal Reflection

Use the exercises below to reflect upon last month and prepare for the month ahead. Also, enjoy "Fun Facts" and share them with your friends!

List 5 things you were GRATEFUL for this month:

1. _____
2. _____
3. _____
4. _____
5. _____

CHALLENGE yourself! Check out these ideas:

Talk to someone new in class and see what you both have in common.

****

Read the news and learn about world events.

Share these FUN FACTS with a friend today:

- Fingernails and toenails counteract the forces put on your feet and hands when you step on or grab different objects.

- North Korea and Cuba are the only places where you can't buy Coca-Cola.

- There are neurons in the stomach, so people really can go with their gut.

- Komodo dragons have bones lining their scales called "bone chainmail." Some scientists believe this is solely to protect these lizards from other komodo dragons.

THINK ABOUT

- What went well last month?
- What could have gone better?
- What did I learn?
- What will I do differently?

B.I.N.G.O.

WAYS TO STAY FOCUSED IN CLASS

Cross off each box after you've tried a new strategy!

Use the 20/5/5 study skill from your MoteNote	Use colored pens to take notes	Engage your eyes, ears, hands, and heart as you learn	Doodle geometric shapes	Add symbols and arrows to your notes
Touch your fingertips together for 1 minute	Flip a negative thought into a positive thought	Be curious, ask questions	Draw meaningful symbols or pictures while reading	Underline keywords in notes, instructions, and word problems
Get permission to chew gum or suck on mints	Circle important dates and names while reading	★	Smile for 15 seconds straight	Squeeze a stress ball
List 3 reasons that it is great to be your age	Study with a friend	Use sticky notes to brainstorm ideas	Draw a picture with 3 details from today's lesson	Imagine how it FEELS to be someone else
Highlight main ideas from an assignment, article, or textbook	Play with thinking or SCENTsory putty	Wiggle your toes to stay alert	Track evidence and examples as you read	Highlight details in class assignments
Make a list of things you're grateful for	Record homework in your MoteNote	Snap pictures of assignments to remember the details	See how many times you can finish the phrase, "I can..."	Choose a seat at the front of your classroom

Feeling Anxious or Stressed?

Quiet the noise around you.

Take 3 slow, deep breaths.

Think 3 positive thoughts.

Be kind to yourself.

Do you feel like you're always being watched?

Don't worry, it's normal to feel that way. Like a fish in a bowl, teens feel like they're being watched all the time, even when they're not being watched at all. It's true – right? This natural phenomenon is called the FISHBOWL EFFECT. It can lead to unnecessary stress, worry, and pressure. Don't buy into it!

Be Smart. Be You. Be Real.
You got this!

Doodles

Month:

Sunday	Monday	Tuesday	Wednesday

Thursday	Friday	Saturday

▶ To Do:

▶ Reminders:

Visual Snapshot of Your Week

KNOW how you spend time? Track your days. SEE **the truth!**

	Get Ready for School	Morning School	Lunch Break	Afternoon School	Homework	Dinner Break and Leave for Soccer	Soccer Practice	Go Home, Wind Down	Sleep

Example — | 6 | 7 | 8 | 9 | 10 | 11 | 12 | 1 | 2 | 3 | 4 | 5 | 6 | 7 | 8 | 9 | 10 | 11 | 12 |

Sunday — | 6 | 7 | 8 | 9 | 10 | 11 | 12 | 1 | 2 | 3 | 4 | 5 | 6 | 7 | 8 | 9 | 10 | 11 | 12 |

Monday — | 6 | 7 | 8 | 9 | 10 | 11 | 12 | 1 | 2 | 3 | 4 | 5 | 6 | 7 | 8 | 9 | 10 | 11 | 12 |

Tuesday — | 6 | 7 | 8 | 9 | 10 | 11 | 12 | 1 | 2 | 3 | 4 | 5 | 6 | 7 | 8 | 9 | 10 | 11 | 12 |

Wednesday — | 6 | 7 | 8 | 9 | 10 | 11 | 12 | 1 | 2 | 3 | 4 | 5 | 6 | 7 | 8 | 9 | 10 | 11 | 12 |

Thursday — | 6 | 7 | 8 | 9 | 10 | 11 | 12 | 1 | 2 | 3 | 4 | 5 | 6 | 7 | 8 | 9 | 10 | 11 | 12 |

Friday — | 6 | 7 | 8 | 9 | 10 | 11 | 12 | 1 | 2 | 3 | 4 | 5 | 6 | 7 | 8 | 9 | 10 | 11 | 12 |

Saturday — | 6 | 7 | 8 | 9 | 10 | 11 | 12 | 1 | 2 | 3 | 4 | 5 | 6 | 7 | 8 | 9 | 10 | 11 | 12 |

Monthly Personal Reflection

Use the exercises below to reflect upon last month and prepare for the month ahead. Also, enjoy "Fun Facts" and share them with your friends!

List 5 things you were GRATEFUL for this month:

1. _____
2. _____
3. _____
4. _____
5. _____

CHALLENGE yourself! Check out these ideas:

Start each day by telling someone you care about, "Good morning!"

****

Listen to music without lyrics while doing your homework.

Share these FUN FACTS with a friend today:

- Dopamine, oxytocin, and serotonin are known as "happy hormones."

- Because there is no atmosphere in space, sound can't travel, and outer space is noiseless.

- Dragonflies are males, damselflies are females.

- October (octo=8) is the 10th month because in 45 BCE, January and February were added to the calendar. January became the first month because the God Janus represents beginnings and endings.

THINK ABOUT

What went well last month?

What could have gone better?

What did I learn?

What will I do differently?

Meal Tracker

Food affects your mood and health. Jot down what you eat this week. Each day, rate how you feel by coloring in the stars.

	Breakfast	Snack	Lunch	Snack	Dinner
Sunday ☆☆☆☆☆					
Monday ☆☆☆☆☆					
Tuesday ☆☆☆☆☆					
Wednesday ☆☆☆☆☆					
Thursday ☆☆☆☆☆					
Friday ☆☆☆☆☆					
Saturday ☆☆☆☆☆					

Think Before You Act

Is this a WISE decision? You'll know by listing the pros and cons.

PROS	CONS

What You See on SOCIAL MEDIA

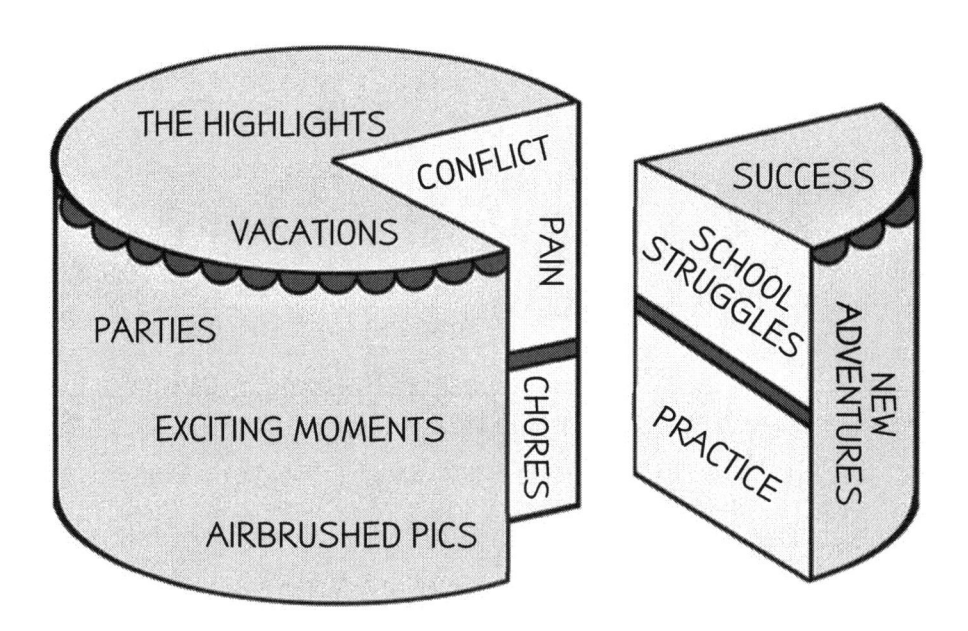

Cake (slice cut out):
- THE HIGHLIGHTS
- VACATIONS
- PARTIES
- EXCITING MOMENTS
- AIRBRUSHED PICS
- CONFLICT
- PAIN
- CHORES

Slice:
- SUCCESS
- SCHOOL STRUGGLES
- NEW ADVENTURES
- PRACTICE

is just ICING on the cake!

Movies to Watch

- Remember the Titans
- Lion
- I Am Eleven

Month:

Sunday	Monday	Tuesday	Wednesday

Thursday	Friday	Saturday

▶ To Do:

▶ Reminders:

Visual Snapshot of Your Week

KNOW how you spend time? Track your days. SEE the truth!

Activities (in order):
- Get Ready for School
- Morning School
- Lunch Break
- Afternoon School
- Homework
- Dinner Break and Leave for Soccer
- Soccer Practice
- Go Home, Wind Down
- Sleep

Example: 6 | 7 | 8 | 9 | 10 | 11 | 12 | 1 | 2 | 3 | 4 | 5 | 6 | 7 | 8 | 9 | 10 | 11 | 12

Sunday: 6 | 7 | 8 | 9 | 10 | 11 | 12 | 1 | 2 | 3 | 4 | 5 | 6 | 7 | 8 | 9 | 10 | 11 | 12

Monday: 6 | 7 | 8 | 9 | 10 | 11 | 12 | 1 | 2 | 3 | 4 | 5 | 6 | 7 | 8 | 9 | 10 | 11 | 12

Tuesday: 6 | 7 | 8 | 9 | 10 | 11 | 12 | 1 | 2 | 3 | 4 | 5 | 6 | 7 | 8 | 9 | 10 | 11 | 12

Wednesday: 6 | 7 | 8 | 9 | 10 | 11 | 12 | 1 | 2 | 3 | 4 | 5 | 6 | 7 | 8 | 9 | 10 | 11 | 12

Thursday: 6 | 7 | 8 | 9 | 10 | 11 | 12 | 1 | 2 | 3 | 4 | 5 | 6 | 7 | 8 | 9 | 10 | 11 | 12

Friday: 6 | 7 | 8 | 9 | 10 | 11 | 12 | 1 | 2 | 3 | 4 | 5 | 6 | 7 | 8 | 9 | 10 | 11 | 12

Saturday: 6 | 7 | 8 | 9 | 10 | 11 | 12 | 1 | 2 | 3 | 4 | 5 | 6 | 7 | 8 | 9 | 10 | 11 | 12

Monthly Personal Reflection

Use the exercises below to reflect upon last month and prepare for the month ahead. Also, enjoy "Fun Facts" and share them with your friends!

List 5 things you were **GRATEFUL** for this month:

1. _____
2. _____
3. _____
4. _____
5. _____

CHALLENGE yourself! Check out these ideas:

Instead of texting your friends when you arrive at their house, stop in and say "Hi" to their parents.

****

Replace all sugary drinks with water next week.

Share these **FUN FACTS** with a friend today:

- An octopus has 3 hearts and 9 brains.

- Nicaragua and Dominica are the only countries with purple in their flags.

- The scientific term for a brain freeze is "sphenopalatine ganglioneurolgia".

- Ever wonder what the difference between poison and venom is? Poison can only be transferred through touch, inhalation, or consumption, while venom must be injected.

THINK ABOUT

What went well last month?

What could have gone better?

What did I learn?

What will I do differently?

My WISE Mind Tells Me To…

Be Kind

Be Accountable

Be a Good Friend

Learn from My Mistakes

Have Compassion for Others

We All See the World Uniquely.
This is <u>PERSPECTIVE</u>.

We can look at the <u>same</u> object and see <u>different</u> perspectives.

What do you see?
What does your friend or sibling see?

There is always more than one perspective.
Try to see things from different perspectives.

Respect differences.

Pause. Look BEYOND Yourself!

Consider ways you can contribute to your...
FAMILY | FRIENDS | NEIGHBORHOOD | SCHOOL | WORLD

Be Mindful

ADD ON | COLOR | SHADE | TRACE | RELAX

Month:

Sunday	Monday	Tuesday	Wednesday

Thursday	Friday	Saturday

▶ To Do:

▶ Reminders:

Visual Snapshot of Your Week

KNOW how you spend time? Track your days. SEE the truth!

	Get Ready for School	Morning School	Lunch Break	Afternoon School	Homework	Dinner Break and Leave for Soccer	Soccer Practice	Go Home, Wind Down	Sleep

Example — | 6 | 7 | 8 | 9 | 10 | 11 | 12 | 1 | 2 | 3 | 4 | 5 | 6 | 7 | 8 | 9 | 10 | 11 | 12 |

Sunday — | 6 | 7 | 8 | 9 | 10 | 11 | 12 | 1 | 2 | 3 | 4 | 5 | 6 | 7 | 8 | 9 | 10 | 11 | 12 |

Monday — | 6 | 7 | 8 | 9 | 10 | 11 | 12 | 1 | 2 | 3 | 4 | 5 | 6 | 7 | 8 | 9 | 10 | 11 | 12 |

Tuesday — | 6 | 7 | 8 | 9 | 10 | 11 | 12 | 1 | 2 | 3 | 4 | 5 | 6 | 7 | 8 | 9 | 10 | 11 | 12 |

Wednesday — | 6 | 7 | 8 | 9 | 10 | 11 | 12 | 1 | 2 | 3 | 4 | 5 | 6 | 7 | 8 | 9 | 10 | 11 | 12 |

Thursday — | 6 | 7 | 8 | 9 | 10 | 11 | 12 | 1 | 2 | 3 | 4 | 5 | 6 | 7 | 8 | 9 | 10 | 11 | 12 |

Friday — | 6 | 7 | 8 | 9 | 10 | 11 | 12 | 1 | 2 | 3 | 4 | 5 | 6 | 7 | 8 | 9 | 10 | 11 | 12 |

Saturday — | 6 | 7 | 8 | 9 | 10 | 11 | 12 | 1 | 2 | 3 | 4 | 5 | 6 | 7 | 8 | 9 | 10 | 11 | 12 |

Monthly Personal Reflection

Use the exercises below to reflect upon last month and prepare for the month ahead. Also, enjoy "Fun Facts" and share them with your friends!

List 5 things you were <u>GRATEFUL</u> for this month:

1. _____
2. _____
3. _____
4. _____
5. _____

<u>CHALLENGE</u> yourself! Check out these ideas:

Every time you are bored this week, write out why you feel that way. Is there a correlation going on?

****

Reconnect with a friend.

Share these <u>FUN FACTS</u> with a friend today:

- The hashtag symbol "#" is an octothorpe because it has 8 points.

- The proper way to list adjectives is by amount, value, size, temperature, age, shape, color, origin, and material.

- Liberia, Burma, and the U.S. are the only countries who use the imperial system.

- A googolplex (1 x 10 10^100) is so large, it's impossible to write it all out as it would require more space than is available in the known universe.

THINK ABOUT

<u>What went well last month?</u>

<u>What could have gone better?</u>

<u>What did I learn?</u>

<u>What will I do differently?</u>

When Did You Last...

Laugh		Cry	
Go out		Stay in	
Spoil Yourself		Spoil others	
Relax		Sleep well	
Get upset		Organize something	
Exercise		Drink water	
Get sick		Play a game	
See a friend		Help a friend	
Stay up late		Sleep in	
Teach someone		Learn something	
Make others laugh		Feel empowered	
Compliment someone		Get complimented	
Clean your room		Call a friend	
Get bored		Daydream	

In Extra-Ordinary Times...
Be EXTRAORDINARY!

Extraordinary people are always pushing themselves. In the space below, jot down ways you can challenge yourself to grow.

The difference between insecurity and confidence is simply <u>PRACTICE</u>.

People You Admire

Write down the names of people you admire and why you admire them in the boxes below. Think of people you know and those you have never met (cultural icons, etc.).

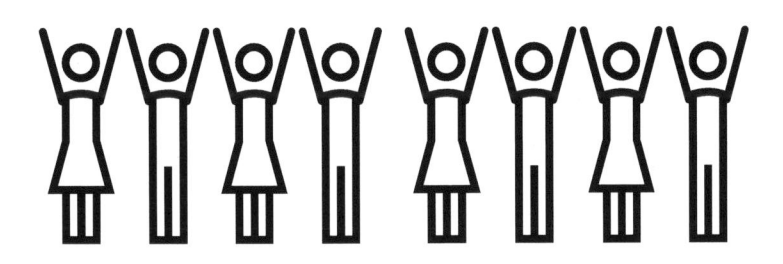

Example: Anne Frank	
I admire Anne for being courageous and hopeful through adversity.	

Month:

Sunday	Monday	Tuesday	Wednesday

Thursday	Friday	Saturday

▶ To Do:

▶ Reminders:

Visual Snapshot of Your Week

KNOW how you spend time? Track your days. SEE the truth!

	Get Ready for School	Morning School	Lunch Break	Afternoon School	Homework	Dinner Break and Leave for Soccer	Soccer Practice	Go Home, Wind Down	Sleep

Example — | 6 | 7 | 8 | 9 | 10 | 11 | 12 | 1 | 2 | 3 | 4 | 5 | 6 | 7 | 8 | 9 | 10 | 11 | 12 |

Sunday — | 6 | 7 | 8 | 9 | 10 | 11 | 12 | 1 | 2 | 3 | 4 | 5 | 6 | 7 | 8 | 9 | 10 | 11 | 12 |

Monday — | 6 | 7 | 8 | 9 | 10 | 11 | 12 | 1 | 2 | 3 | 4 | 5 | 6 | 7 | 8 | 9 | 10 | 11 | 12 |

Tuesday — | 6 | 7 | 8 | 9 | 10 | 11 | 12 | 1 | 2 | 3 | 4 | 5 | 6 | 7 | 8 | 9 | 10 | 11 | 12 |

Wednesday — | 6 | 7 | 8 | 9 | 10 | 11 | 12 | 1 | 2 | 3 | 4 | 5 | 6 | 7 | 8 | 9 | 10 | 11 | 12 |

Thursday — | 6 | 7 | 8 | 9 | 10 | 11 | 12 | 1 | 2 | 3 | 4 | 5 | 6 | 7 | 8 | 9 | 10 | 11 | 12 |

Friday — | 6 | 7 | 8 | 9 | 10 | 11 | 12 | 1 | 2 | 3 | 4 | 5 | 6 | 7 | 8 | 9 | 10 | 11 | 12 |

Saturday — | 6 | 7 | 8 | 9 | 10 | 11 | 12 | 1 | 2 | 3 | 4 | 5 | 6 | 7 | 8 | 9 | 10 | 11 | 12 |

Monthly Personal Reflection

Use the exercises below to reflect upon last month and prepare for the month ahead. Also, enjoy "Fun Facts" and share them with your friends!

List 5 things you were **GRATEFUL** for this month:

1. _____
2. _____
3. _____
4. _____
5. _____

CHALLENGE yourself! Check out these ideas:

Drive without music. Focus on driving and the things around you.

****

Take a 30 minute walk with a friend this week.

Share these **FUN FACTS** with a friend today:

- Before women could vote, in 1916, Jeannette Rankins was the first U.S. Congress Woman.

- Koala fingerprints are so similar to humans that police have mistaken them for human prints at crime scenes.

- The same hormone (DHT) that supports a full beard also causes male-pattern baldness.

- Cold welding is when two pieces of the same metal touch in space and fuse together due to the lack of atmosphere.

THINK ABOUT

What went well last month?

What could have gone better?

What did I learn?

What will I do differently?

Reach Your Goals

Write your goal on the top of the ladder. Then on the rungs of the ladder write steps, or habits, that will lead to your goal.

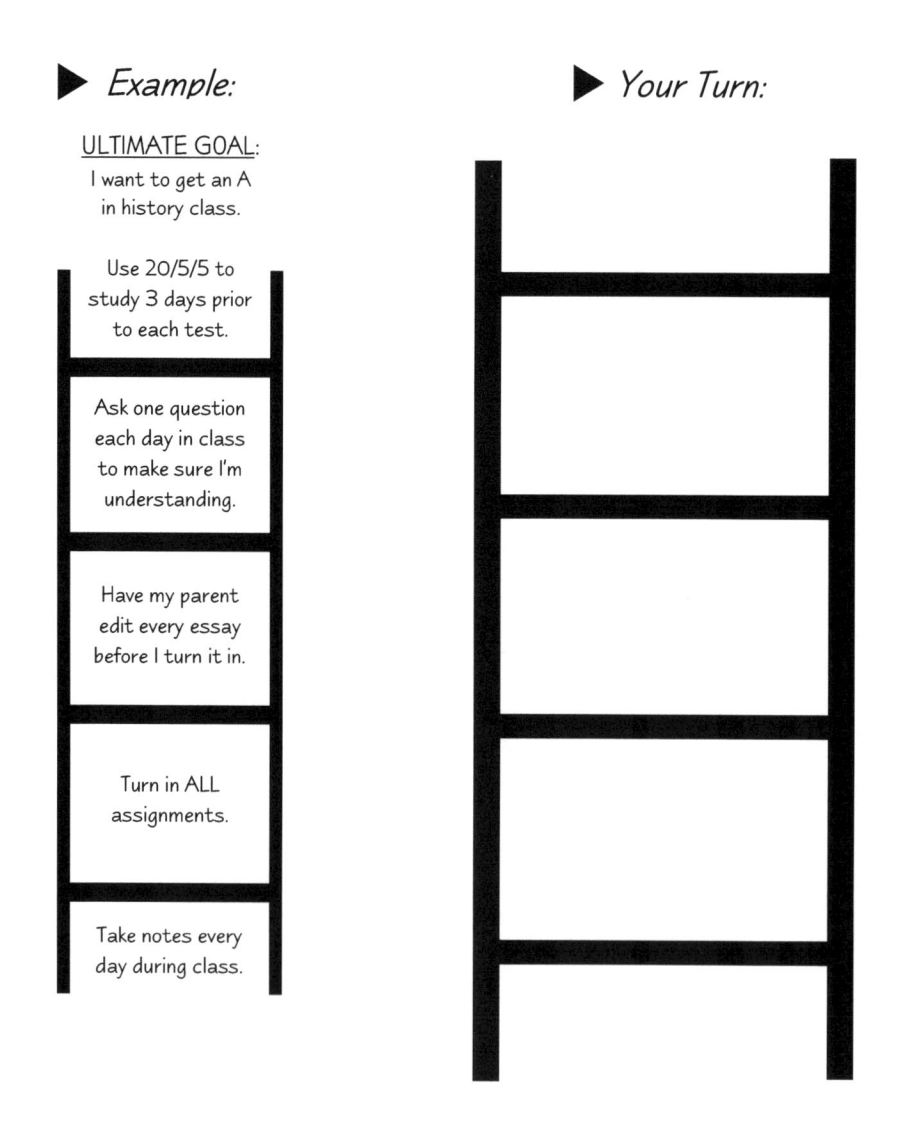

▶ *Example:*

ULTIMATE GOAL:
I want to get an A in history class.

Use 20/5/5 to study 3 days prior to each test.

Ask one question each day in class to make sure I'm understanding.

Have my parent edit every essay before I turn it in.

Turn in ALL assignments.

Take notes every day during class.

▶ *Your Turn:*

Want to change your mood?
Change your thinking!

Science says thinking positive thoughts for 5-minutes improves your mood as much as a 20-minute walk!

Hard to believe? Try it for yourself!

Out of 5 stars, rate how you feel RIGHT NOW.

☆☆☆☆☆

Then, set a timer for 5 minutes and write down as many positive things as you can. They don't have to be real - anything positive will work.

After the timer goes off, rate how you feel NOW.

☆☆☆☆☆

Now, try this with a 20-minute walk.

Rate how you feel BEFORE the walk: Rate how you feel AFTER the walk:

☆☆☆☆☆   ☆☆☆☆☆

Now do you believe?

"Look for a way to lift someone up. And if that's all you do, that's enough."

-Elizabeth Lesser

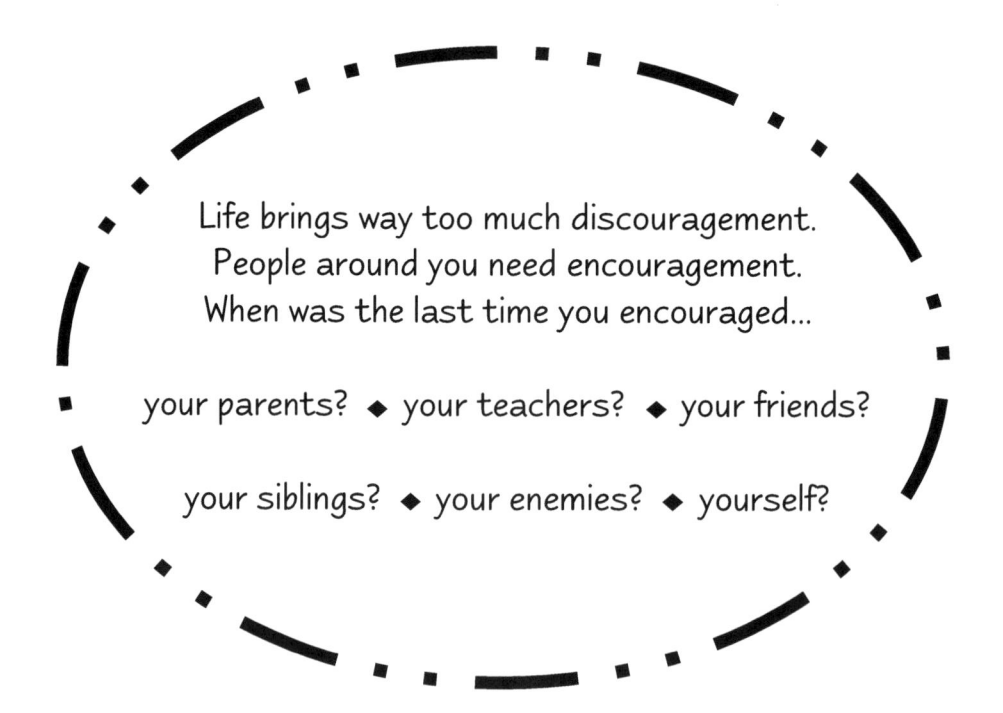

Life brings way too much discouragement.
People around you need encouragement.
When was the last time you encouraged...

your parents? ◆ your teachers? ◆ your friends?

your siblings? ◆ your enemies? ◆ yourself?

Great Books to Read

Jot down titles of books that people recommend to you. Get inspired and learn something new through someone's story.

- Wonder
- Among the Hidden
- Catch-22
- 1984
- Lord of the Flies
- Educated

Month:

Sunday	Monday	Tuesday	Wednesday

Thursday	Friday	Saturday

▶ To Do:

▶ Reminders:

Visual Snapshot of Your Week

KNOW how you spend time? Track your days. SEE **the truth!**

	Get Ready for School	Morning School	Lunch Break	Afternoon School	Homework	Dinner Break and Leave for Soccer	Soccer Practice	Go Home, Wind Down	Sleep

Example — | 6 | 7 | 8 | 9 | 10 | 11 | 12 | 1 | 2 | 3 | 4 | 5 | 6 | 7 | 8 | 9 | 10 | 11 | 12 |

Sunday — | 6 | 7 | 8 | 9 | 10 | 11 | 12 | 1 | 2 | 3 | 4 | 5 | 6 | 7 | 8 | 9 | 10 | 11 | 12 |

Monday — | 6 | 7 | 8 | 9 | 10 | 11 | 12 | 1 | 2 | 3 | 4 | 5 | 6 | 7 | 8 | 9 | 10 | 11 | 12 |

Tuesday — | 6 | 7 | 8 | 9 | 10 | 11 | 12 | 1 | 2 | 3 | 4 | 5 | 6 | 7 | 8 | 9 | 10 | 11 | 12 |

Wednesday — | 6 | 7 | 8 | 9 | 10 | 11 | 12 | 1 | 2 | 3 | 4 | 5 | 6 | 7 | 8 | 9 | 10 | 11 | 12 |

Thursday — | 6 | 7 | 8 | 9 | 10 | 11 | 12 | 1 | 2 | 3 | 4 | 5 | 6 | 7 | 8 | 9 | 10 | 11 | 12 |

Friday — | 6 | 7 | 8 | 9 | 10 | 11 | 12 | 1 | 2 | 3 | 4 | 5 | 6 | 7 | 8 | 9 | 10 | 11 | 12 |

Saturday — | 6 | 7 | 8 | 9 | 10 | 11 | 12 | 1 | 2 | 3 | 4 | 5 | 6 | 7 | 8 | 9 | 10 | 11 | 12 |

Monthly Personal Reflection

Use the exercises below to reflect upon last month and prepare for the month ahead. Also, enjoy "Fun Facts" and share them with your friends!

List 5 things you were **GRATEFUL** for this month:

1. _____
2. _____
3. _____
4. _____
5. _____

CHALLENGE yourself! Check out these ideas:

Eat with chopsticks. If you don't know how, then have a friend teach you.

****

Use a sticky note to keep track of tasks for the day.

Share these **FUN FACTS** with a friend today:

- The Gambia and The Bahamas are the only countries with the word "The" in their titles.

- A human typically carries 10 times more bacterial cells than human cells.

- Harry Potter was translated into Ancient Greek for students studying the language.

- The website Google got its name from 'Googol'= 10^{100}, a number named by Edward Kasner when he asked his 9 year old nephew, "What would you call a huge number?"

THINK ABOUT

- What went well last month?
- What could have gone better?
- What did I learn?
- What will I do differently?

Think Before You Act - Take 2*

Is this a WISE decision? You'll know by listing the pros and cons.

PROS	CONS

*Since this is such a vital tool, it's in your MoteNote twice!

Things that Brighten Your Day

In the sun rays, jot down things that make you happy!

Happy Brain = Healthy Life
DOODLE | DRAW | CREATE | COLOR | EXPRESS | FOCUS

Favorite Family Traditions

In the space below, write down your favorite family traditions and why they are meaningful to you.

Draw pictures, use color, and reflect on memories!

ACADEMIC STUDY SKILLS

Your HAPPY Brain
Study Skill for Emotional Health

Have these four items at hand to ensure a positive study session:

1. A *slightly* sugary beverage
2. A healthy snack
3. An item that makes you happy
4. A PLAN for your study session

*Don't forget to use the 20 / 5 / 5 study skill to stay focused! See the next page for more information.

20 / 5 / 5

A Study Skill for Time Management, Focus, and Memory

20 min: DO

Your brain learns best when it chunks down time and tasks. Spend 20 minutes reading, studying a chunk of info, or completing part of a task. Focus! After all, it's only 20 minutes!

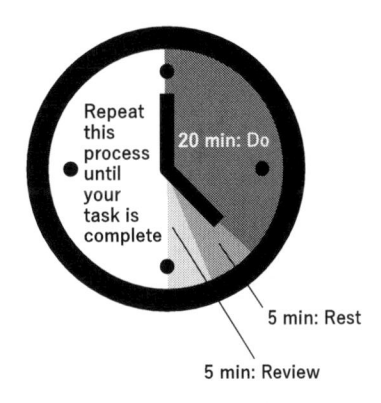

5 min: REST

*Take a **short** break and let your brain rest for 5 minutes. Your brain is highly active when it rests because it organizes, sorts through, and makes connections between prior knowledge and new information. Get a snack, listen to a song, take a short walk, or throw a ball. But only for 5 minutes!*

5 min: REVIEW

Then, review what you learned in the first 20 minutes. Challenge your brain to remember as much as possible.

↻ *Then,* **REPEAT** *this process with the next chunk of info or part of a task!*

P.Q.R.S.T.
Study Skill for Reading Comprehension

P = Preview
Preview the material before you read. Notice titles, subtitles, bold words, pictures and captions, charts, etc. Make connections to your prior knowledge.

Q = Questions
Read any **questions** before you read the text. Circle and underline keywords.

R = Read
Use your hands as you **read**. Underline, circle, highlight, and use symbols to categorize information.

S = Summarize
As you read, stop frequently and use your own words to **summarize** each section.

T = Test
Test yourself. Answer the questions using the text to help you. Then check your answers!

Mind Movie

Study Skill for Deeper Comprehension

Bring your learning to life by imagining yourself in the time and place of the information you are learning about.

Engage your senses by picturing yourself seeing, tasting, hearing, smelling, touching, and emotionally connecting with the content. Your Mind Movie will continually evolve as your knowledge grows!

P.E.E.

Study Skill for Writing Essays

Use this simple structure to write clear, focused responses

P = Point
Brainstorm 2 or 3 main points you already know about your topic. Follow each main point with an example and explanation.

E = Example
Examples can be quotes, statistics, or personal stories.

E = Explain
Explanations connect your example to your point.

Finally, write an introduction and conclusion to sandwich in your P.E.E., and you are all set!

G.U.T.A.C.

Study Skill for Math Word Problems

Math word problems got you stumped?
Remember G.U.T.A.C. to get you over the hump!

Given	What information are you **given** in the problem? Circle it.
Unknown	What **unknown** information do you need to find? Underline it.
Tools	What **tools** can you use to help you find the unknown info? (equation, picture, proportion, chart, etc.)
Answer	Find the **answer**!
Check	Make sure your answer is right by asking if it makes sense and by **checking** your equation or picture.

P.O.E.
Study Skill for Test-Taking

Use this strategy for <u>P</u>rocess <u>O</u>f <u>E</u>limination on tests

1. Circle the key words from the **QUESTION.** You can't answer the question if you don't know what it's asking!

2. You should then be able to eliminate 2 answers. This will leave you with 2 answers left to dissect.

3. Ask yourself what the **DIFFERENCE** is between the 2 remaining answer choices.

4. If you still don't know the answer, often, the more **SPECIFIC** and **DETAILED** answer choice is correct.

5. Finally, if you're still unsure, **SAY** aloud the question paired with each of your two remaining answers. See which answer choice is a better match to the question.

*** For math: Try plugging in each answer and WORKING BACKWARD. One of the choices must be right.*

Expanding Language
Study Skill for Vocabulary

Instead of this...	Say this...
good	fantastic, marvelous, wonderful, spectacular, awesome, extraordinary
bad	inauspicious, disadvantageous, adverse, difficult, inopportune, unpropitious, unfavorable
exciting	thrilling, exhilarating, rousing, electrifying, invigorating, inspiring, gripping, powerful
favorite	dearest, treasured, special, closest to one's heart, pet, preferred, chosen, ideal

HANDY MATH RESOURCES

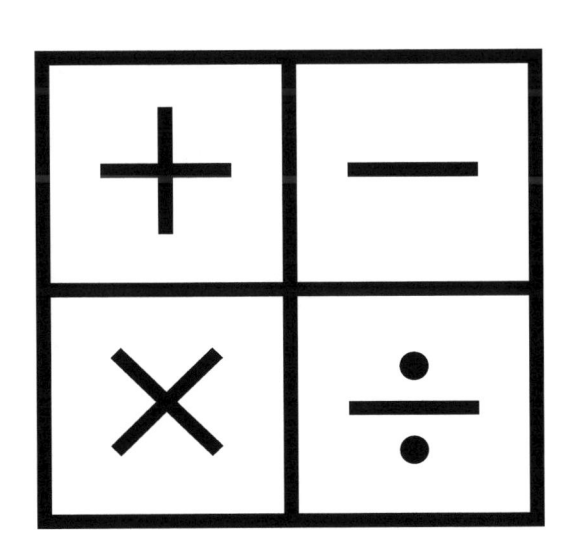

Number Categories

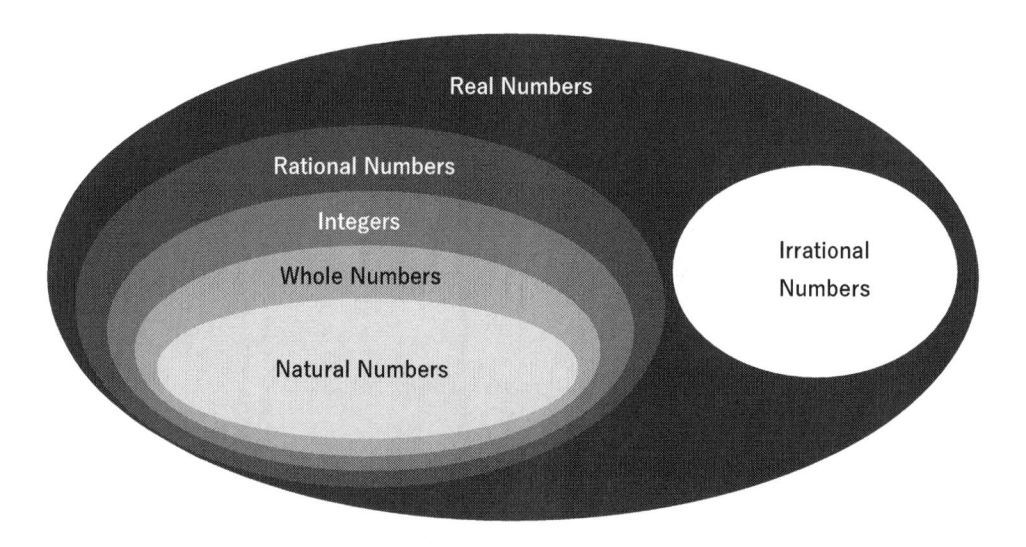

Real Numbers	The combination of all rational and irrational numbers. Think of this as ALL of the numbers. ie. 0.6, 0.123123, π, e, $\sqrt{2}$, $\sqrt{5}$, 1, 2, -1, -2, $\cdots$
Rational Numbers	Any number that can be written as a fraction. These numbers have either finite or repeating decimals. This also includes all integers. ie. ½, 2/3, 0.6, 0.123123
Irrational Numbers	Numbers that can NOT be written as a fraction. These numbers don't have a pattern to their decimals. ie. π, e, $\sqrt{2}$, $\sqrt{5}$, $\cdots$
Integers	All whole numbers and their negatives. ie. $\cdots$, -3, -2, -1, 0, 1, 2, 3, $\cdots$
Whole Numbers	Natural numbers including 0. ie. 0, 1, 2, 3, 4, $\cdots$
Natural Numbers	Your counting numbers starting at 1. ie. 1, 2, 3, 4, $\cdots$

Helpful Math Vocab

Vocab Word:	Definition	Example:
Factor	Values that divide a large or equal known number	Factors of 25: 1,5,25 Factors of 32: 1,2,4,8,16,32
Variable	An unknown placeholder in an expression	Common Variables: x, y, z
Coefficient	A number or quantity multiplied to a variable	In $7x^2 + 5x$, both 5 and 7 are coefficients.
Product	To multiply together	The product of 2 and 9 is 18
Expression	A mathematical phrase that contains numbers and variables	$7x^2 + 5x$
Equation	An expression that contains an equal sign	$y = 7x^2 + 5x$
System of Equations	Multiple equations all related by the same variables or unknowns	$3x + 4y = 10$ $2x + 3y = 7$
Rate of Change	The speed at which a variable changes over time	(graph showing linear increase from 1 to 4)
Domain	All the input values that are either allowed or possible	The domain of the graph above is [1,4]
Range	All of the output values that are possible	The range of the graph above is [2,8]
Acute Angle	An angle less than 90 degrees	(acute angle figure)
Obtuse Angle	An angle greater than 90 degrees and less than 180 degrees	(obtuse angle figure)
Right Angle	An angle that measures exactly 90 degrees	(right angle figure)

When Can You Divide by...

One?   Always!

Two?   When the last digit is even

Three?   When the sum of all the digits is divisible by 3

Four?   When the number is divisible by 2, twice

Five?   When the last digit is 0 or 5

Six?   When the number is divisible by 2 AND 3

Seven?   See next page...

Eight?   When the number is divisible by 2, thrice

Nine?   When the sum of all the digits is divisible by 9

Ten?   When the last digit is a 0

When Can You Divide by the...

TRICKY 7?

Rule:	Examples:	
	Works:	Doesn't work:
To check if a number is divisible by 7, remove the last digit from the number and subtract it from the remaining digits twice. If your new number is divisible by 7, then your original number is divisible by 7.	581 =>58 and 1 58-1=57 57-1=56 56 IS divisible by 7 so 581 is also divisible by 7. 5355 =>535 and 5 535-5=530 530-5=525 (we can repeat the process to see is 525 is divisible by 7) 525 => 52 and 5 52-5=47 47-5=42 42 IS divisible by 7 so 525 is divisible by 7, AND 5355 is divisible by 7.	729 =>72 and 9 72-9=63 63-9=54 54 IS NOT divisible by 7 so 729 is not divisible by 7. 4985 => 498 and 8 498-8=490 490-8=472 (we can repeat the process to see if 472 is divisible by 7) 472 => 47 and 2 47-2=45 45-2=43 43 is NOT divisible by 7 so 472 is not divisible by 7, AND 4985 is not divisible by 7

Common Conversions

Volume

1 fl oz = 29.574 mL
1 pt = 0.473 L
1 qt = 0.946 L
1 gal = 3.785 L

1 mL = 0.034 fl oz
1 L = 2.113 pt
1 L = 1.057 qt
1 L = 0.264 gal

Length

1 in = 2.54 cm
1 ft = 30.48 cm
1 yd = 0.914 m
1 mi = 1.609 km

1 mm = 0.039 in
1 cm = 0.394 in
1 m = 1.094 yd
1 km = 0.621 mi

Weight

1 oz = 28.350 g
1 lb = 0.454 kg
1 g = 0.035 oz
1 kg = 2.205 lbs

1 ton = 2,000 lbs
1 metric ton = 1,000 kg
1 ton = 0.907 metric tons
1 metric ton = 1.102 ton

Quadrilateral Flow Chart

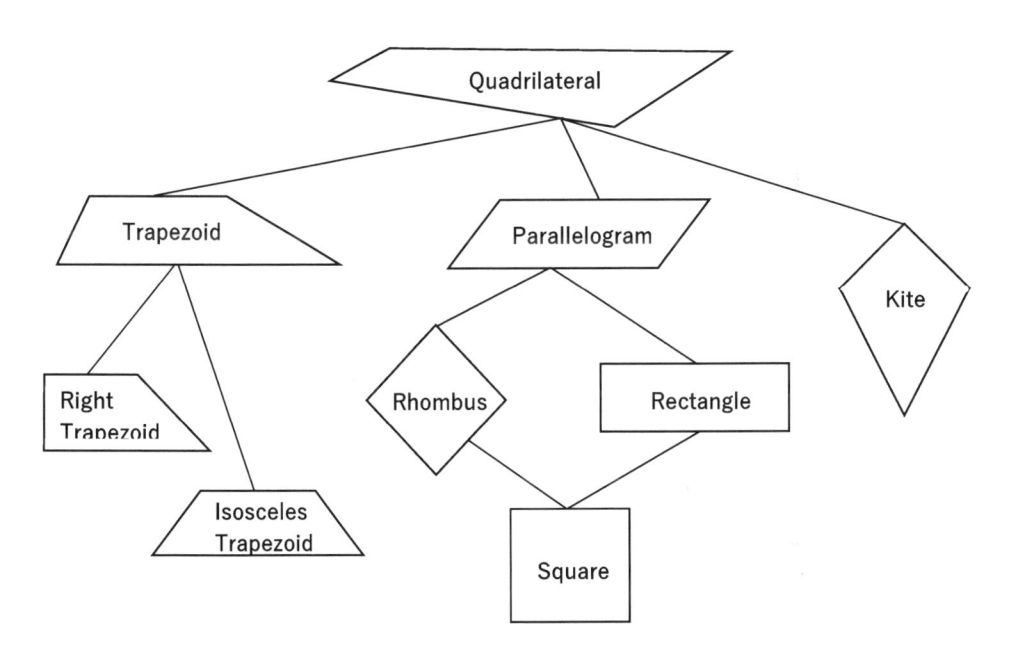

Quadrilateral	A 4 sided figure
Trapezoid	A quadrilateral with exactly 1 pair of parallel sides
Parallelogram	A quadrilateral with 2 pairs of parallel sides
Kite	A quadrilateral with 2 pairs of 2 adjacent equivalent sides
Right Trapezoid	A trapezoid with 1 right angle
Isosceles Trapezoid	A trapezoid whose two unparallel sides are equal length
Rhombus	A parallelogram whose sides are all equal length
Rectangle	A parallelogram with only right angles
Square	A rectangle that is also a rhombus

Made in the USA
Columbia, SC
04 April 2021